The Peace Rose

Written and Illustrated
by
Alicia Olson

A division of Montessori Services
www.montessoriservices.com

Dedicated to
the children of Leelanau Montessori

ISBN # 978-0-939195-34-3 (Paperback Edition)
ISBN # 978-0-939195-55-8 (Hardcover Edition)
Library of Congress Control Number: 2017906653

Originally published under the name Alicia Jewell

Printed in Korea
Reprinted 2018, 2022

A division of Montessori Services
www.montessoriservices.com

In a special place in our room

we have a peace rose.

When we have a problem

the rose helps us

talk about our feelings.

Once, John and William

both started to paint

at the same time.

They went to get the peace rose

and they took turns talking.

"William, I felt sad when you wanted

to paint at the same time.

Please let me go first."

"Okay, John. I'm sorry.

Please tell me when you're finished."

"Friends!"

13

Another time, Hannah took Jacob's block.

He said, "You're not my friend anymore."

She went to the peace shelf to get the rose

and they took turns talking.

"Jacob, I felt hurt when you said,

'You're not my friend anymore.'

Please don't say that."

19

"Okay, Hannah.

But I felt angry when you grabbed my block.

Please ask first."

"Friends!"

You can even solve a problem

without using a rose.

Like the time Heather pushed Jackie.

The two girls took turns talking.

"Heather, I felt mad when you pushed me.

Please keep your hands to yourself."

"Okay, Jackie.

I'm sorry."

"Friends!"

A TEACHER'S GUIDE TO THE PEACE ROSE

In response to children's almost daily interpersonal conflicts, teachers are often tempted to scold the children for using negative language or to make a questionable judgment as to which child is in the wrong. The Peace Rose offers an alternative that will free you from this no-win situation by enabling the disputing children to calmly express their feelings to each other and reach an amicable agreement on their own.

Because the procedure with the Peace Rose teaches children to recognize and communicate their feelings, as well as to listen to another child express his or her feelings, it introduces children as young as three to basic problem-solving techniques. After using this activity in their classroom, some children even employ their new peacemaking skills in problem situations outside their classroom community.

Introducing the Peace Rose to Your Students

During the first month of the school year, tell your class that you are going to show them a new way to resolve a conflict with another person. Put a lovely silk rose into a small vase and place it on a low shelf that the children can easily reach. "This is our Peace Rose," you can say, "and it is very special. We keep it here on the shelf, and when we want to use it, we hold it very carefully." Show them how to hold it in front of them and then pass it around so each child can take it gently and hold it as you did.

Next, ask another adult to role-play the following scenario with you. Begin by pretending you are having an argument. Then, say that you want to use the Peace Rose and take it carefully from the shelf. While holding it in front of you:

Say the other adult's name: "Joseph ..."

Describe your feelings: "I feel sad because ..."

Tell him what caused your feelings: "...you took my pencil without asking me."

Name what you would like to be different: "Please ask me if you want to use my pencil."

Then give the Peace Rose to your role-playing partner who says your name, describes his feelings, and says what he would like to change:

"Lauren, I was mad because you took my red crayon. I want you to give me back my red crayon."

He returns the Peace Rose to you and you say: "Here is your red crayon. I'm sorry I took it."

Hand the Peace Rose to your partner. He says: "Thank you, Lauren. Next time I will ask you first if I want to use your pencil."

Then together you both hold the Peace Rose and say, "We are friends" or just "Friends."

You can then practice this same scenario with several children, one at a time. Eventually, the children will be able to do it without your assistance.

Teacher's Support for the Peace Rose

The Peace Rose is not intended to be a shameful sign or a punishment for a child's misbehavior. It is simply a tool that the children use like any other material in the classroom.

When children involved in a conflict want you to settle their dispute, you can ask, "Would you like to use the Peace Rose?" If the answer is "Yes," you can ask "Would you like some help?" If the children are experienced in the process, they usually decline assistance. You can then simply observe from a distance to ensure they are following the procedure correctly.

If they indicate that they would like your help, you can prompt them to address each other by name, describe their feelings, and indicate what they would like to change. Your role is to assist the children through the process. Do not force the children to apologize to each other, as a forced apology is never genuine. However, suggesting an apology is not out of place.

When one child expresses his feelings and the other fails to respond, you can break the awkward silence by saying, "You don't have to apologize, but your friend must know that you heard him." Let the child know he may say, "I heard what you told me," or "That's okay, (name)."

You may find that sometimes students go back and forth repeating the details of their disagreement without expressing their feelings and moving on. It is then necessary for you to intervene by reminding each child to say how she feels and then bring the dialog to closure.

As you speak respectfully to each child, your manner serves as a model for them to speak respectfully to each other. Remind them that they may not use insulting phrases like "You're mean" or "You're bad." They may only express their own feelings. Such statements are called "I messages" and can be useful to them throughout their lives.

Personal peace, peace in families and peace among nations are goals shared by human beings everywhere. The question is always where to begin. The internationally known educator, Maria Montessori, once corresponded with the great peacemaker Mahatma Gandhi who agreed with her that " ... if we want peace in the world ... we must begin with the children."

No one is claiming that the Peace Rose will ultimately lead to a peaceful world, but it can lead children to reject violent means of settling disputes. If our youngest citizens form the habit of resolving conflicts peacefully, it is possible they will become more peaceful adults who, hopefully, will work toward a more peaceful world.

The Peace Shelf

On page 16, the illustration shows a Peace Shelf with materials intended to foster peace in the classroom. Here are some ideas for materials that could be found on a Peace Shelf.

Peace Cards. Written commands and pictures encouraging actions of peace and friendship. The child selects a card, reads the command and carries it out. Examples include:"Hug a friend." and "Smile."

Small Peace Pole. A symbol of peace that can be used in place of the Peace Rose or in any other peace activity.

Zen Garden. A miniature rock garden with sand and small tools that the children can use for creating a peaceful scene.

Joy and Sorrow Boxes. Two boxes, each containing pencils and paper. The children may draw and write about things that make them happy, then fold the paper and place it in the Joy Box. Children may also draw or write about things that make them sad and put those drawings into the Sorrow Box.

Peace Mat. A soft square of fabric for a child to sit on, and a small, comforting object to hold, such as a small, smooth crystal or stone carving. This is useful for a child who needs time to cool off in a special place.

Gift-Making Materials. Simple items for the children to use to make gifts for friends and family. Suggestions for this activity include beads to make bracelets or necklaces and heart cut-outs for writing "love notes."

Feelings Cards and Mirror. These cards are simply photos of children expressing various emotions such as anger, happiness, and sadness. The mirror can be used by the child to see his own face showing these emotions. (These cards can be purchased commercially or made by photographing your students in the classroom expressing different emotions.)

Feelings Cards Matching Game. Two sets of cards depicting various emotions for the children to match.